Thank you to God for this inspiration and creating beauty from ashes.

I feel so blessed and grateful to my wonderful husband, Jim and my beautiful boys Zachary and Matthew. You fill me with hope, joy and love every day.

My wish....
Anyone in a relationship with Doubt can understand doubt is really a covering over their greatest strengths.

I hope this book inspires people to let go of their friendship with Doubt and see the beauty of the gifts God sent them here to enjoy.

Before I made my trip from heaven to earth, God helped me pack an amazing treasure chest to take with me. The contents were for me to wear. In the treasure chest was:

Strength

Love

Wonder

Peace

Joy

Gentleness

They were all in the form of beautiful invisible gowns.

While we packed, God held my face in His hands and told me, "You are my beautiful child. I created you to wear these gowns every day. They will sparkle, shine, vibrate and glow." I felt so loved, comforted, content and beautiful. The gowns were just right for me. As I tried them on, I felt their invisible power radiate from the inside to the outside.

As I experienced life on earth, I realized some people did not like me wearing my gowns. They did not like them. So often times I got hurt or insulted when I wore them. I began to feel ashamed of my gowns like they were not meant for me. Not right for me. Something must be wrong with me. I was not sure what to do or how to handle people's reactions to my gowns.

Then I met what I thought was an amazing and protective friend. This friend's name was **Doubt**. She saw my invisible gowns but thought it would be best to hide them. She shielded me from sharing them so I would not be hurt.

Doubt guarded me from disappointments, being let down and from having to be courageous when difficult things needed to be done.

Doubt was always there.

Doubt was the cloak over my gowns of:

Strength

Love

Wonder

Peace

Joy

Gentleness

I stayed safe.

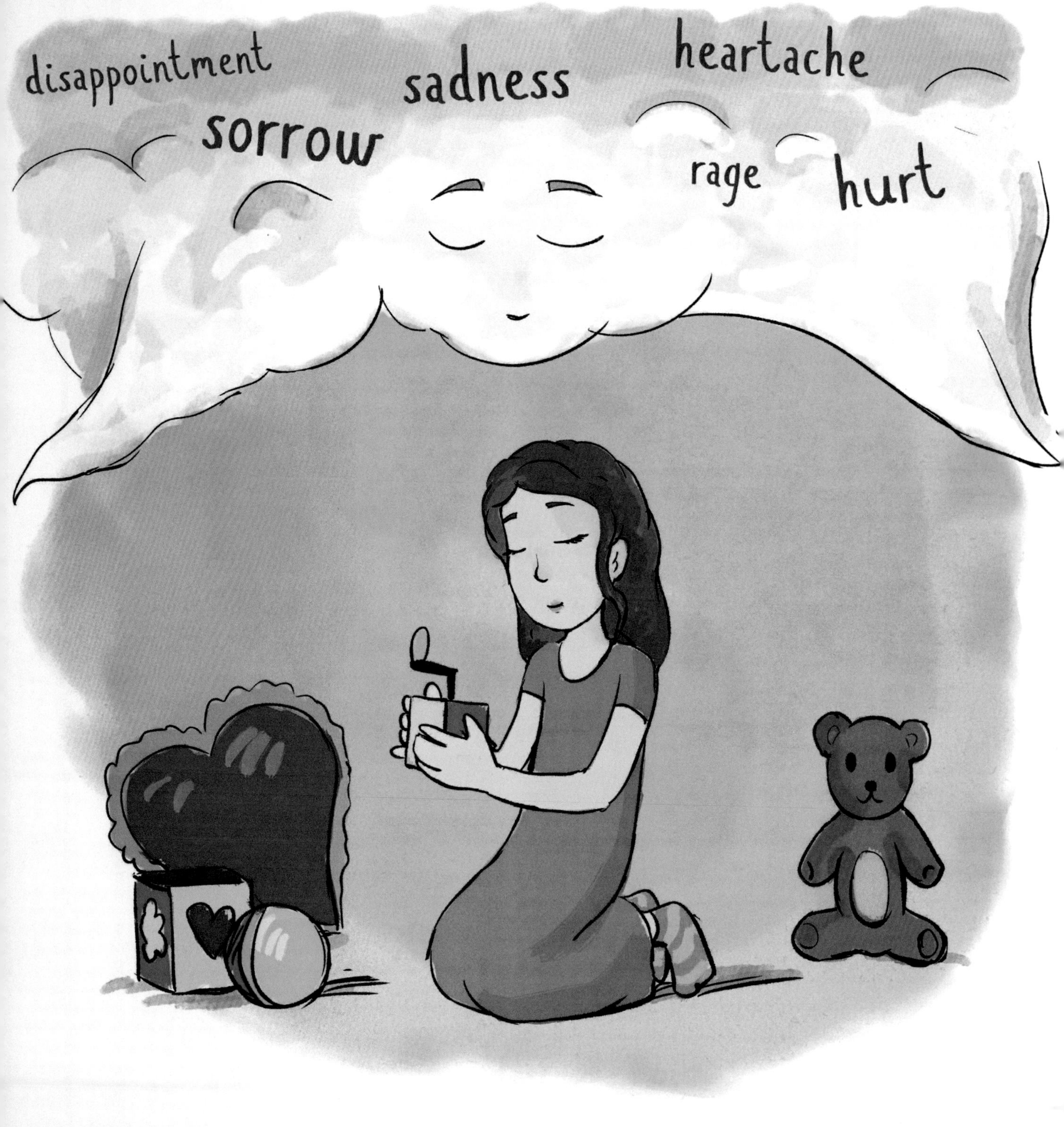
disappointment
sorrow
sadness
heartache
rage
hurt

When I thought I had Strength in my Strength gown, **Doubt** would say, "I don't think so." She guarded me. She would say "No way, run, you are not that strong, other people are stronger than you. You can't handle this. You are weak."

When I was feeling
Love in my Love
gown, and opening
myself to receive
other's love,
Doubt would
shield me and say
"I do not think they
love you---they
want something."

When I would feel love in my heart for others, **Doubt** would tell me "It will not last or it is not safe or worth it. The cost is a lot of pain!"

When I would be in my Wonder gown and in awe during miraculous events, **Doubt** would keep me safe by telling me, "Focus only on the facts and only believe in your physical senses." **Doubt** would tell me "You do not live in a fantasy world. Dreams don't come true."

When I would wear my Peace gown, **Doubt** would step in front of me and tell me to not let down my guard. She would tell me, "Danger is around every corner. Peace is the calm before the storm." She would tell me, "Be prepared...always."

When I would wear my Joy gown, **Doubt** would simply warn me that it will not last. She would tell me, "This Joy gown vibrates and calls too much attention to you...it is not a good idea... Not safe."

When I wore my Gentleness gown, that is when **Doubt** would guard me the most. Doubt would say "It is not safe, too vulnerable for attack and you will be too exposed and too open."

I know **Doubt** thought she was doing what was best for me, especially during my childhood and growing up. Exposing my beautiful gowns of Strength, Love, Wonder, Peace, Joy and Gentleness simply was not safe. They were not understood or cherished.

I am forever grateful to **Doubt**. She was helpful for a time.

As I matured, my friendship with **Doubt** began to change. I started to develop relationships with other friends and teachers that told me I had beautiful gowns. I was surprised they could see my invisible gowns. They saw them because they had them too. I was able to see their invisible gowns. These people were changing the world. I wanted to change the world too.

The longing to completely experience the fullness of the amazing and beautiful gowns of *Strength*, *Love*, *Wonder*, *Peace*, *Joy* and *Gentleness* was overcoming me. I began to have an aching that there was more to my life than to have **Doubt** always with me.

Doubt realized she was no longer needed and it was time for her to change. Doubt began to gradually transform herself to become an even better friend—**Hope.**

Now that I am maturing, the fog of Doubt is clearing and exposing the truth that these gowns fit me perfectly.

I now have **Hope**. I realize I am big enough and strong enough and know who gave me these amazing and beautiful gowns in the first place.

My gowns are God's gifts for me to experience and cherish and to share. It is so wonderful to be with my new friend **Hope** and to wear these gowns of *Strength, Love, Wonder, Peace, Joy* and *Gentleness* every day. I know they are my special treasures from God and amazing gifts to be shared with others.

As I wear these gowns now, sometimes Doubt still visits, we then decide it is better to have **Hope** by my side. Now I allow the gowns vibrations to fill me and I trust God's promises and remember His words to me, "You are my beautiful child! I created you to wear these gowns every day."

10489943R00026

Made in the USA
Lexington, KY
24 September 2018